Bud Bud the Wonder Horse

By Greg Huett

Dedicated to my four sons Wilson, Austin, Hayden and Joseph. Like Bud Bud, these young men can do about anything. And like Bud Bud, they realize they are always welcome and safe in their Father's unconditional love and presence, no matter where life takes them.

Published in 2018 by Big Country Farm Toys, LLC

ISBN 978-1-7324897-8-3

Printed in China.

The illustrations were created by Gideon Burnett and the story was written by Greg Huett.
Based on the actual farm animals from the Huett family farm.

For more information about Big Country Farm Toys and the Huett family farm, visit www.bigcountryfarmtoys.com

But the father said to his servants, "Bring quickly the best robe, and put it on him, and put a ring on his hand, and shoes on his feet. And bring the fattened calf and kill it , and let us eat and celebrate. For this my son was dead, and is alive again: he was lost, and now he is found." And they began to celebrate.

Luke 15:22-23

Farmer Jay has an amazing farm.

There are all kinds of animals on his farm and each of them has a special job to do.

The sheep are being sheared so their wool can be used to make clothing for Farmer Jay and his family. Their long wool made them hot in the summer. But the sheep were thankful to be part of Farmer Jay's farm.

The hens are laying eggs in their nest so the farmer and his family will have food for their table. It seems like a lot of work and even painful, but the chickens were thankful to be a part of Farmer Jay's farm.

The cows line up to be milked. Their milk would be used to make cheese for the farmer and his family. It takes a lot of milk to make a pound of cheese. But the cows were thankful to be a part of Farmer Jay's farm.

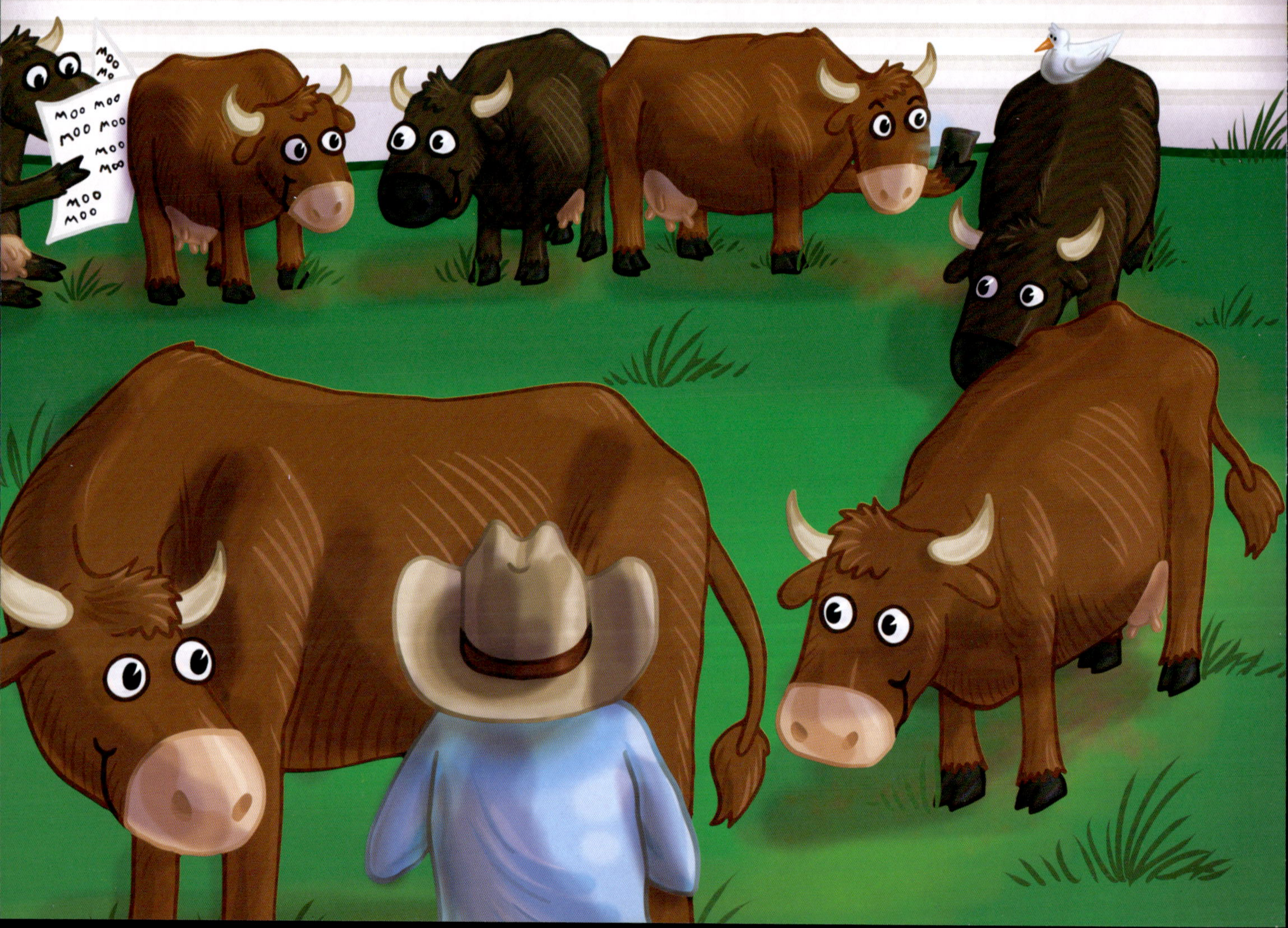

And Farmer Jay's farm had a horse. His name is Bud Bud. Everybody called him Bud Bud the Wonder Horse. He got his name because Bud Bud was no ordinary horse.

He could pull a wagon.

He could herd cattle.

He could compete in the rodeo.

And he was even the star of the Main Street parade.
You see, Bud Bud could do anything.

And the farmer loved Bud Bud.

He had his own special stall.
He always got fed first.
He had his own halter and blanket.
Farmer Jay loved Bud Bud the Wonder Horse.
And Bud Bud loved being part of the farm.

But one day, Bud Bud decided that he was far too valuable to be working on one small farm. And the work on the farm was too much work for a horse of his ability. So Bud Bud decided he would run away to a farm that didn't require so much work. He heard there was a farm like this on the other side of the hill. While everyone was sleeping, Bud Bud jumped the fence and ran as fast as he could away from Farmer Jay's farm.

And when he got to this farm, he found it just as he had hoped.

The chickens didn't have to lay eggs.

The sheep didn't grow wool.

The cows didn't get milked and Bud Bud didn't have to ride anyone or pull anything. Bud Bud loved being a part of this new farm.

Back at Farmer Jay's farm, with Bud Bud being away, the other animals were having to do Bud Bud's chores.

They didn't like pulling wagons and plows and starring in rodeos and parades.

But it wasn't long before Bud Bud realized that since no one had to work, there wasn't anything for anyone to eat. And Bud Bud got so hungry that he began to think about his life on Farmer Jay's farm. He thought about his stall and his blanket and most of all about having all the grain he could eat.

He longed to be back home at Farmer Jay's farm. But how could he ever go back? He had been so wrong for running away. How could Farmer Jay forgive him?

He couldn't sleep all night, so he decided it was time to go back to Farmer Jay's farm. All the way home he thought about how mad Farmer Jay must be and he wondered if he would ever let him come back to his farm to stay.

But as he turned into the road leading to the farm, he looked up and saw, much to his surprise, there was Farmer Jay running to meet him. He hugged Bud Bud the Wonder Horse and called for his farm hands to bring him a new halter and blanket and take him to his stall so he could eat all the grain that he wanted.

The next day, all the other farm animals asked Farmer Jay how he could celebrate Bud Bud's return after how he had left them.

Farmer Jay got all the animals around him. And he told them, "I celebrated because I thought Bud Bud was lost or dead and now he's come home. You see, sometimes we have to be away from home and those who love us to realize how good we have it and how badly we need them. And isn't it good to know we can always come home no matter where we have been or what we have done?"

That night Bud Bud the Wonder Horse lay in his stall with his new halter and blanket and all his farm friends and realized how good it really is to be a part of Farmer Jay's farm.

We hope you have enjoyed Bud Bud the Wonder Horse. For some extra fun, go back and try to find the doves we have placed along the way, in various places in the story. You should be able to find all **21**. You can find additional books along with farm, ranch and rodeo toys on our website at www.bigcountryfarmtoys.com.

Check out some of the actual farm animal characters living on the Huett farm:

Baby Timmy

Timmy

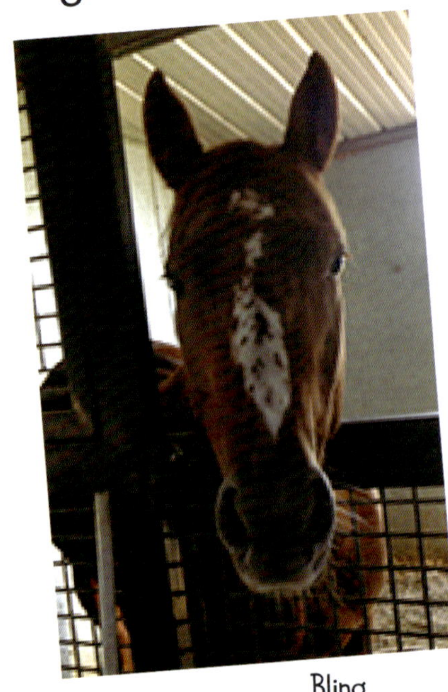

Bling

Timmy

Scan the QR code to learn more about Bud Bud the Wonder Horse and the other animals on the Huett farm.

Greg and Bling

Ellie

Big Sway

Clovie Jean and Hayden

Bud Bud

Big Red

Bud Bud and Hayden

Scan the QR code to learn more about Bud Bud the Wonder Horse and the other animals on the Huett farm.

Scarlet

Minnie Ruth

Benny

Lucy

Woodrow

Baby Woodrow

Laurie Darling

Scan the QR code to learn more
about Bud Bud the Wonder Horse
and the other animals on the Huett farm.